Beloved Forever

In Loving Memory

A Journal of Remembrance

I Dedicate This Journal
In Loving Memory and Honor Of

_____

_____

_____

Beloved Forever

In Loving Memory

A Journal of Remembrance

Written by Gloria Jelladian
California

Journal Cover Design
Interior Book Design
by
JelladianArt.com

ISBN 0963650602

*"When you are sorrowful
look again in your heart,
and you shall see that in truth
you are weeping for that
which has been your delight."*
~ *Khalil Gibran*

"Wounds of the spirit are most gently soothed and made whole by the passing years. Under the old scars flows again the calm, healthful tide of life. Under a great loss the heart impetuously cries that it can never be happy again, and perhaps in its desperation says that it wishes never to be comforted. But though angels do not fly down to open the grave and restore the lost, the days and months come as angels with healing in their wings. Under their touch aching regret passes into tender memory; into hands that were empty new joys are softly pressed; and the heart that was like the trees stripped of its leaves and beaten by winter's tempests is clothed again with the green of spring." ~ *George S. Merriam*

Introduction

"My prayer is that this special journal will be your comforting companion while writing your heartfelt memoirs. Honor the love and the phases of your story in this important journey. Write from the clouds. Write your authentic and sincere words from your heart and it will help you to explore and express your deep feelings of your truth. Writing your thoughts and feelings will help you to add a new level to your relationship with your beloved. Preserve your cherished reflections and treasured sentiments in this invaluable keepsake journal. And behold the priceless blessings of your writing and healing journey into peace and gracious harmony." ~ Gloria

~ Photo ~

*"Our beloved's pure unconditional love for us
gives us the strength to carry on."*
~ Ralph Jelladian

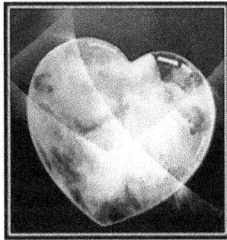

The Mighty Redwood Among The Pines
By Gloria Jelladian

Poem Written in Honor of Gloria's
Beloved Cousin Carey Ann

The mighty redwood, towering above the pines, never yields in the cold winter's snow... nevertheless capable of tenderly enjoying the gentleness of a soft spring rain, embracing the affection of the giving summer sun, and inhaling the life-giving majestic beauty of a glorious rainbow. The mighty redwood, sturdily planted deep within the fertile soil of Mother Earth, stands strong in relentless fierce winds and lightning bolts from heaven above. The mighty redwood holds the light; she shades the weak, and transgresses the unyielding wrath of Mother Nature's fury. And the mighty redwood with rings and rings of eternity, holding the wisdom of the ages for eons and eons of time, also comes to a transition after a fruitful and generous life. Following a life of standing tall and taking all of the harshness that

Mother Nature dished out, the mighty redwood falls and lays in sacred rest. Sustenance from what was within the mighty redwood nourishes sweet splendid treats, adding magnificence to the life cycle of cosmic glory, continuing the successions of metamorphosis of nature's divine flow in evolution. Like life and energy, there is no death... only the celestial transitioning of Crystalline Love.

~ Photo ~

"I thought of you with love today,
but that is nothing new.
I thought about you yesterday,
and days before that, too.
I think of you in silence,
I often speak your name.
All I have are memories
and your picture in a frame.
Your memory is my keepsake,
with which I'll never part.
God has you in his keeping,
I have you in my heart!
Forever and Always."
~ Author Unknown

"Goodbyes are only for those who love with their eyes. Because for those who love with heart and soul there is no such thing as separation."
~ Rumi

"Those we Love remain with us,
for Love itself lives on.
Cherished memories never fade
because a loved one is gone.
Those we Love can never be
more than a thought apart.
For as long as there is a memory,
they'll live on in our heart."
~ Author Unknown

~ Photo ~

"Being deeply loved by someone gives you strength, while loving someone deeply gives you courage."
~ Lao Tzu

~ Photo ~

*"I was standing in our dining room
thinking of nothing in particular,
when a cablegram was put into my hand.
It said, 'Susy was peacefully released today.'
It is one of the mysteries of our nature that a man,
all unprepared, can receive a
thunder-stroke like that and live."*
~ Mark Twain

"Death comes to all,
but great achievements build
a monument which shall endure
until the sun grows cold."
~ Ralph Waldo Emerson

*"Only people who are capable of loving strongly
can also suffer great sorrow,
but this same necessity of loving serves to
counteract their grief and heals them."*
~ Leo Tolstoy

"Here bring your wounded hearts,
here tell your anguish.
Earth has no sorrow
that Heaven cannot heal."
~ Thomas Moore

"LOVE is something that won't ever fade.
Once you really love someone,
that person will stay
in your heart forever."
~ Author Unknown

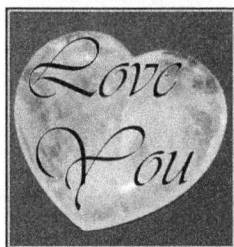

"When someone you love becomes a memory,
the memory becomes a treasure."
~ Author Unknown

"Blessed are those who mourn,
for they will be comforted."
~ Matthew 5:4

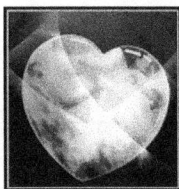

"We bereaved are not alone. We belong to the
largest company in all the world...
the company of those who
have known suffering."
~ Helen Keller

"Death leaves a heartache no one can heal.
Love leaves a memory no one can steal."
~ From a headstone in Ireland

"There are things that we don't want
to happen, but have to accept.
Things we don't want to know,
but have to learn.
And people we can't live without,
but have to let go."
~ Author Unknown

*"While grief is fresh, every attempt
to divert only irritates.
You must wait till it be digested,
and then amusement will
dissipate the remains of it."*
~ Samuel Johnson

*"Thankfulness brings you to
the place where the Beloved lives."*
~ Rumi

"I thought I could describe a state;
make a map of sorrow.
Sorrow, however, turns out to be
not a state but a process."
~ C.S. Lewis

"Within tears, find hidden laughter.
Seek treasures amid ruins, sincere one."
~ Rumi

*"To weep is to make less
the depth of grief."*
~ William Shakespeare

"Friends....
They cherish one another's hopes.
They are kind to one another's dreams."
~ Henry David Thoreau

"Everyone copes differently.
Some cry for the loss of a loved one.
Others smile because they know
they will see them again."
~ Author Unknown

"Sadness flies away on the wings of time."
~ Jean de la Fontaine

"Let's be grateful for those who give us happiness;
they are the charming gardeners
who make our soul bloom."
~ Marcel Proust

*"Cultivate the habit of being grateful
for every good thing that comes to you,
and to give thanks continuously.
And because all things have contributed to
your advancement, you should include
all things in your gratitude."*
~ Ralph Waldo Emerson

"Tis better to have loved and lost
than never to have loved at all."
~ Lord Tennyson

LOVE TO PRAY — feel often during the day the need for prayer and take trouble to pray. Prayer enlarges the heart until it is capable of containing God's gift of Himself. Ask and seek, and your heart will grow big enough to receive Him and keep Him as your own.

"Keep the joy of loving God in one another and share this joy with others. God Bless You."
~ Mother Teresa

Dear Gloria,

Thank you for your kind get-well card
and for your prayers and wishes for
my recovery from my recent illness.

I am deeply touched at your kindness
and I ask God to fill you with His
blessings - you and your family. Keep
the joy of loving God in one another
and share this joy with others.

God bless you
lle Teresa Me

"Back in 1989, when I had read in the local newspaper that Mother Teresa had health issues, I mailed a get well card to Mother in Calcutta, India. To my surprise, she wrote me this beautiful thank you letter. I am happy to share with you the personal letter that I received from our Beloved Mother Teresa. Embrace the Love and Blessings."

"Yesterday is gone.
Tomorrow has not yet come.
We have only today.
Let us begin."
~ Mother Teresa

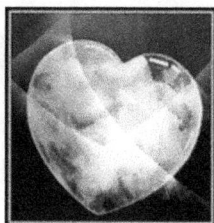

"It is in dying that we are
born to eternal life."
~ St. Francis of Assisi

"The pain passes, but the beauty remains."
~ Pierre Auguste Renoir

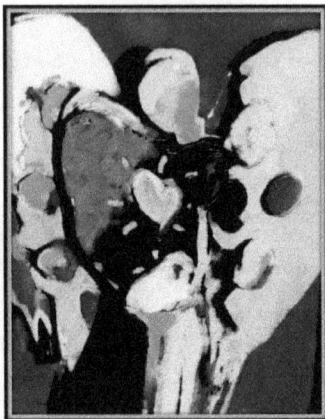

"*Everyone has a Guardian Angel
given to them from the beginning.
Belief and faith is what we need to
feel and hear them in our heart.
In peaceful silence… listen….
Feel the Love. Enjoy the Bliss.*"
*~ Gloria Jelladian
Angelmaker/Sculptor*

"Love Fearlessly....
Endlessly... and Forever."
~ Gloria Jelladian

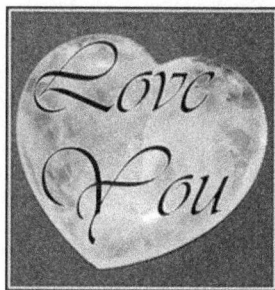

www.ingramcontent.com/pod-product-compliance
Lightning Source LLC
Chambersburg PA
CBHW051753040426
42446CB00007B/352